Welcome to the Corinium Museum

This is the fourth Museum in Cirencester to bear this name and continues a tradition reaching back over 150 years. The present Museum was completely refurbished and redisplayed between 2002 and 2004 to create an exciting experience for both adults and children and to accommodate the huge volume of archaeological discoveries made since the 1970's. We have written this booklet partly as a guide to the displays and the history of the Cotswolds but also as a souvenir of your visit.

Cirencester stands at the junction of three major Roman roads and contains some of the most important archaeological remains from Roman Britain. With the exception of London, it boasts the largest concentration of mosaics from this country (over 90 are known from the town), the remains of a Roman theatre, a basilica and forum and one of the largest and best preserved amphitheatres in the country. As a result, the Corinium Museum houses one of the finest collections of Roman antiquities in the country.

"In my opinion the Corinium Museum, at the centre of one of the richest regions of Roman Britain, contains a collection of pre-eminent value, whether viewed from international, national or regional perspectives." Professor Sheppard Frere (Emeritus Professor of the Archaeology of the Roman Empire, University of Oxford).

The Corinium Museum, however, is more than a Roman museum. It houses many other amazing treasures from the Cotswolds. It tells the story of the Cotswolds from the earliest hunter-gatherers to the canals and railways of the industrial revolution!

We do hope you enjoy your visit and will come back to see us again soon.

Dr. John Paddock
Curator of Museums

Fragment of a Medieval stone statue depicting a young woman's or angel's head, late 13th/early 14th century, from Cirencester Abbey.

Accession number 1980/79/28

The Hare Mosaic. This mosaic is unique in Romano British archaeology in that the central roundel depicts a hare, an animal sacred to the Celts. The mosaic was discovered during excavations of an elaborate late 4th century town house in Beeches Road, Cirencester. The discovery of the mosaic coincided with the first major redevelopment on this site and caused such a stir archaeologically, that the Hare Mosaic became synonymous with the Corinium Museum and has been its logo ever since.

Accession number T22

Prehistory

A time before history

Prehistory is the name given to the period of human existence before written records. It spans the period that saw the human way of life change from that of nomadic hunter-gatherers to farmers living in settled communities. To make this vast period of time more understandable, archaeologists have divided it into the Stone Age, the Bronze Age and the Iron Age, based on changes in the technology used to manufacture tools and weapons.

A handaxe or bi-face found during gravel extraction in South Cerney, near Cirencester. This tool is over a quarter of a million years old. It was carefully fashioned from a nodule of flint into a hand-held multi purpose tool for chopping and cutting.

Accession number 1976/363

A group of flint microliths and scrapers which date from the Mesolithic period. Microliths were assembled together to form composite tools like the reconstructed arrow heads shown here.

The Earliest Inhabitants

The Old Stone Age or the Palaeolithic period covers a vast span of time from when we first have evidence of our earliest ancestors about 700,000 years ago, until about 12,500 years ago. For most of that time Britain was not an island, but part of a larger European landmass and for long periods covered by glaciers. Our ancestors followed and hunted large herds of animals. During cooler times these could be reindeer and woolly mammoth, and during warmer times, horse, deer and rhino.

In the Cotswolds, the earliest evidence we have for human presence is from handaxes, a multi-purpose tool for chopping and cutting, which are believed to be about 200,000 to 300,000 years old. Most of the handaxes in the area have been found during gravel extraction at the Cotswold Water Park, near Poole Keynes and South Cerney, although others have also been found at Meysey Hampton, Fairford, Lechlade, Bourton-on-the-Water and Moreton-in-Marsh.

The Hunter Gatherers

About 12,500 years ago Britain became an island. Our ancestors were now gatherers as well as hunters, and roamed around far smaller territories than before. The period from then until about 6,000 years ago is known as the Mesolithic period or Middle Stone Age.

Handaxes and other large implements were supplemented by tools made of small, narrow flint blades or *microliths*. Small concentrations of these microliths have been identified at over 40 sites in the Cotswolds, most notably at Cherington, Whittington and at Hazelton North. These concentrations indicate a more settled way of life with the groups remaining in a single area for longer periods of time.

A group of Neolithic flint leaf shaped arrowheads. Flint does not occur naturally in the Cotswolds and many tons were imported during the Neolithic period. The delicate pressure-flaking and symmetry of these pieces is a tribute to the skill of the flint knapper that made them and belies their purpose, for hunting and war!

The people of the Neolithic period laid out their dead in large burial monuments like the one at Hazleton. The construction of this monument or long barrow was almost certainly a communal effort, it has been estimated that it took about 17,000 hours and certainly indicates a concern for the dead and possibly ancestor worship. This burial mound had 2 chambers and held about 23 bodies. The Museum contains a reconstruction of its south chamber.

The First Farmers

From about 4,000 BC, new ideas and technologies developed across Europe in what we call the New Stone Age or Neolithic period. Tools were still made of stone, but consisted of a wider variety of shapes, including beautifully polished stone axes. The Corinium Museum holds several of these from Cirencester, Driffield, North Cerney, South Cerney and Upper Slaughter.

The most significant development was the domestication of plants and animals. Farming fundamentally changed the human way of life as it could provide a more predictable and sustainable food supply, thus supporting larger populations within a smaller area.

Society became more organised and large settlements were built, such as Crickley Hill near Cheltenham and Cowley Peak near Stroud.

A group of Neolithic stone and flint axes. Stone and flint for axes was also imported but most axes were traded as finished tools. Because the Cotswolds is nearer flint rich areas than the igneous stone rich areas of the Lake District and Cornwall the majority of axes are made of flint.

Prehistory • 4/5

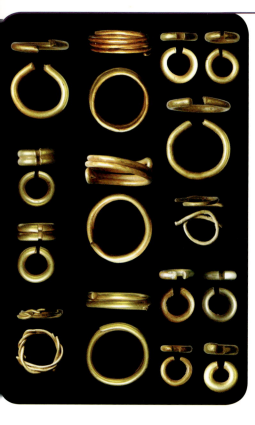

A hoard of gold from Poulton near Cirencester. Was it a goldsmith's hoard or an offering to the gods? This hoard consists of a mixture of complete and deliberately broken items of jewellery which may have been cut up for re-smelting in a crucible or to render them unusable.

Accession number 2007/18

New Materials; the Bronze Age

From about 2500 BC, the use of metals had spread to the Cotswolds. First came copper and then bronze, an alloy of copper and tin, which created a harder more durable cutting edge for tools and weapons. At first, this new technology was used side by side with flint but then tools, weapons and jewellery became increasing specialized and elaborate, suggesting that society had started to divide on the basis of wealth and power.

"A dagger grave?" This striking pair of bronze daggers, of middle Bronze Age date, were found near Fairford. They probably came from a round barrow destroyed by gravel workings. Only the 2 daggers survive so there is no way of telling what sex the owner was. Dagger burials of this type are relatively common in the middle Bronze Age and are clearly indicative of the important social position of the owner.

Accession number 1991/26 and 1991/28

A late Iron Age gold coin or stater probably minted at Bagendon, depicting a triple tailed horse. The horse was clearly important to the Dobunni, and the area around Claydon Pike between Lechlade and Fairford seems to have been used for large-scale horse rearing prior to the Roman Invasion of 43 AD.
Accession number 1982/135

The Cotswolds before Rome

About 700 BC, the peoples of Britain began to use iron rather than bronze for tools and weapons. This was a period of massive population growth and increased social unrest, resulting in changes in the organisation of the land and the construction of many fortified villages or hill forts.

By the 2nd century BC, distinct tribal groups had emerged throughout Britain; the tribe in the Gloucestershire region was called the Dobunni. By the 1st century BC there were already close trading contacts between southern Britain and the continent, stimulating the development and growth of semi-urbanised centres or oppida.

Locally, the most important of these were at Salmonsbury, near Bourton on the Water, and Bagendon, just north of Cirencester. The oppidum at Bagendon was probably the tribal centre for the Dobunni from about 20 AD to 50 AD. Outside such centres, the Dobunni lived in small rural settlements or isolated farmsteads supported by mixed farming.

In the 1st century AD the geographer Ptolemy recorded Britain's main exports as slaves, grain, cattle, gold, silver, iron and hunting dogs. From archaeological evidence we know that its main imports were fine tablewares, wine and other luxury goods from the continent. Large quantities of this imported pottery and wine amphora were found during excavations at Bagendon and "the Ditches", Woodmancote. Excavations of other local sites such as Crickley Hill, Lydney Park, Uley Bury, Salmonsbury and Claydon Pike at Fairford have revealed a sophisticated economy. Salt was widely traded, iron working was generally domestic in scale, but highly skilled travelling smiths undertook bronze working.

The aristocracy of the Dobunni shared the Celtic love of decoration. This can be seen from surviving examples of metal work from Gloucestershire including the beautiful cast bronze and enamelled chariot harness mount found near South Cerney. This object is unique in the incorporation of stylized birds' heads in its design and was probably made in the second quarter of the 1st century AD.

Accession number 1998/93

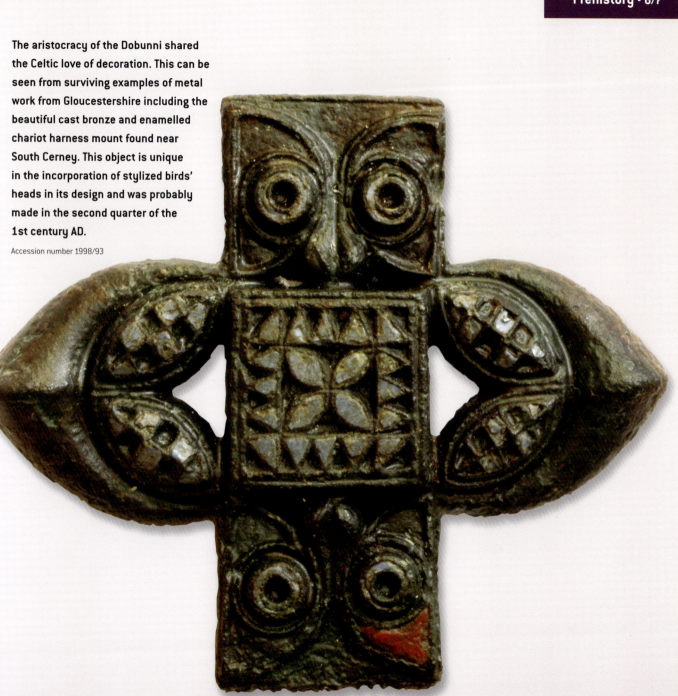

The Romans

The coming of the Romans

Rome's first contacts with Britain were through trade, but during his campaigns in Gaul, the Roman general Julius Caesar led two expeditions to Britain in 55 and 54 BC. These were followed a hundred years later by a full-scale invasion led by the Emperor Claudius. In July 43 AD a Roman army of about 40,000 men landed in Britain. After a lightning campaign Claudius received the surrender of 11 kings and a number of tribes - amongst whom were the Dobunni.

Detail of the Orpheus Mosaic showing a tiger part of the cycle of animals charmed by Orpheus's lyre playing. The mosaic, which dates to the first half of the 4th century AD, depicts Orpheus at its centre encircled by birds and beasts. It was found in 1825 at Barton Farm in Cirencester Park. The worship of Orpheus was one of a number of eastern cults, which promised their followers an afterlife to become popular in the 3rd and 4th centuries AD.

Accession number T25

The Romans • 8/9

A rare set of silvered and decorated saddle plates from Cirencester. These items date to the early 1st century AD and were used to decorate horse harness by Roman cavalry for parade purposes. Like the modern British army there was quite a distinction between "battle dress" and "ceremonial dress".

Accession number 2005/131

Within a year of the conquest, a fort was established on the site of present day Cirencester (at the crossing of the River Churn), 4 kilometres south of the old Dobunnic centre at Bagendon. No visible sign of this fort remains today but we know from excavations that it had turf and timber ramparts with internal timber buildings.

Our evidence for the garrison comes from stray finds of military equipment and two exceptionally fine tombstones found in the Watermoor area of Cirencester in the 19th century. These belonged to Genialis and Dannicus respectively, auxiliary cavalrymen who died on active service in the area. They were provincials recruited from present day Holland and Switzerland respectively.

The Tombstone of Genialis. Tombstones like these give us invaluable information. We can expand the inscription of the Genialis tombstone to read in English:

"Sextus Valerius Genialis, trooper of the (first) cavalry regiment of Thracians, a Frisian tribesman, in the troop of Genialis, aged 40, of 20 years service, lies buried here. His heir had this set up."

This gives us some idea just how cosmopolitan the Roman army had become, Genialis was a Frisian (from Holland) in a unit of Thracians (modern Bulgaria).

Accession number B956

A fragment of an inscription from a major public building in Roman Cirencester, found at the Beeches Road town house. This records the two senior local magistrates the duoviri iuricundi. These elected officials were the equivalent of the consuls in Rome, and were responsible for the administration of justice in Corinium amongst other things.
Accession number 1980/111/15

A Roman garrison remained for over 20 years, until the military situation changed as a result of the Roman conquest of Wales. The presence of so many well paid troops with "money to burn" soon attracted traders and other civilians to the area outside the fort and a village or vicus developed. As the *vicus* grew in importance the Dobunnic centre at Bagendon seems to have declined.

Roman Cirencester

To administer their provinces the Roman government encouraged the establishment and growth of towns. The new province of Britannia was no exception. Here new towns were often laid out on or near the site of the earlier tribal centres and became the administrative hub of their areas. Town councils and magistrates, whose members were drawn from the tribal aristocracy and modelled on those of

Reconstruction of the Forum and Basilica complex as it might have looked at the end of the 2nd century AD. This was the administrative and ceremonial centre of the town and the tribal area. The Basilica, a huge aisled building, housed the records of the administration and hosted the meetings of the ordo (town council). It also served as the law courts. The interior of the building was elaborately decorated with imported marble veneers, mosaic floors and bronze statues.

Reconstruction drawing of Corinium's Verulamium (London Road) gate as it would have looked in the 4th century AD.

The Seasons Mosaic is one of the most impressive pavements ever found in Britain. It depicts the four seasons and scenes from Roman mythology linked with Bacchus, the god of wine. The mosaic was originally composed of nine octagons; each framed a roundel containing a figurative panel. Only three of the seasons, survive: Spring: Flora, goddess of flowers, wearing a garland. Summer: Ceres, goddess of agriculture, carrying a sickle (depicted here) and Autumn: Pomona, goddess of the orchard, carrying a pruning knife.

Rome, were established. These councils were responsible for administering the region, the local law courts and the collection of taxes.

The Roman geographer Ptolemy identifies the new town at Cirencester as Corinium Dobunnorum or "Corinium of the Dobunni". Between the years 80-150 AD a street grid was laid out and all the major public buildings and amenities expected of a major Roman town were developed. These included the Basilica and Forum complex, baths, an amphitheatre and a theatre as well as numerous temples and elaborate town houses.

Corinium was to be the second largest town in Roman Britain; its walls eventually enclosed 96 hectares and it probably had a population of between 10,000 and 15,000. (A comparable figure to modern day Cirencester of around 18,000.)

Monumental gateways were built and a ditch and bank defined the town. Probably in the late 2nd or early 3rd century AD, stone walls were added to the front of the bank.

Pictures in Stone

The Corinium Museum is renowned for its collection of mosaics from the town and the surrounding area. Over 95 mosaics are known from the town. Two of the earliest and the most beautiful and accomplished come from a town house at the lower end of the present market place known today as the Dyer Street town house. These date to the 2nd century AD at the time that the major public buildings were being laid out.

The Romans • 12/13

Another detail from the famous "Seasons" Mosaic, depicting the destruction of the legendary hunter. The scene catches the moment that Actaeon, being transformed into a stag, is devoured by his own hunting hounds as a punishment for having caught a glimpse of the goddess Diana naked in her bath. The quality of this mosaic is quite exceptional and arguably as fine as any ever found in Roman Britain.

Accession number 1983/2

A detail from the "Hunting Dogs" Mosaic depicting the head of Neptune, god of the sea. This vivid and lively depiction was created using tiny tesserae and made use of exotic materials such as red glass and onyx. The mosaic, which dates to the middle of the 2nd century AD, was originally composed of aquatic imagery but was later remodelled to include the hunting dogs, and other unrelated patterns, possibly as a result of the collapse of part of the floor. It was found during drainage works in Dyer Street Crencester in 1849.

Accession number 1983/1

Houses continued to be built and decorated with mosaics throughout the 3rd century AD but it is in the 4th century AD that a group of mosacists set up a "business" in and around Cirencester. Their products divide into two general types, the Orpheus style and the so-called *saltire* style. They flourished in the first half of the century and by the end of Roman Britain many of their products were being patched with *opus signinum*, a type of pink cement, there presumably being no one left with the skill to mend them properly!

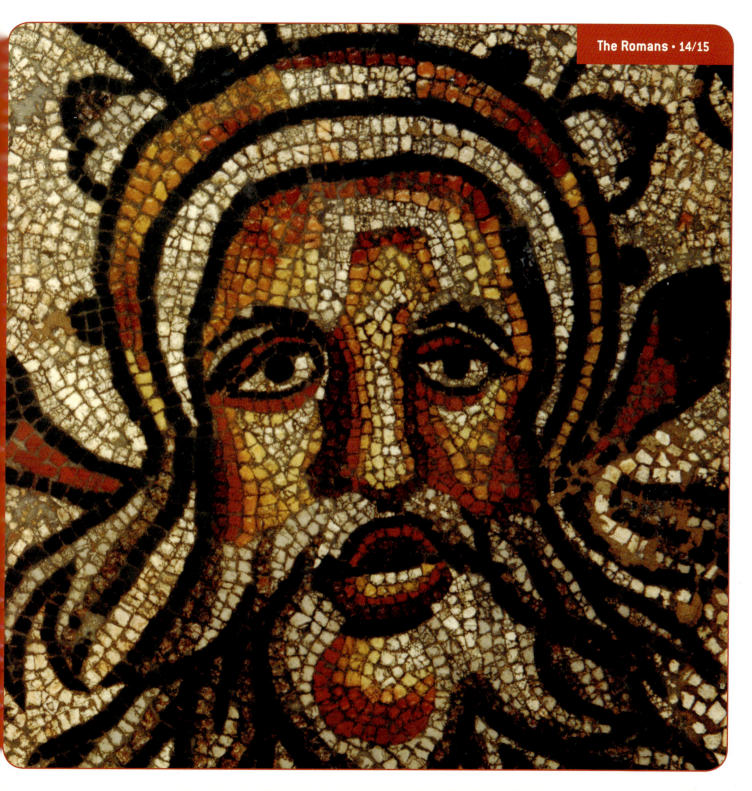

A unique Romano-British Corinthian capital inhabited by four Bacchic figures. It depicts Bacchus (the god of wine), Silenus, a maenad or female follower, and the Thracian King Lycurgus. The capital comes from a free-standing column, which once stood in the centre of Roman Corinium. Found at The Leauses, Cirencester in 1838.

Accession number A348

Gods for All Seasons

The Romans brought the worship of the classical gods, with them to Britain, particularly Jupiter, Juno and Minerva. Jupiter and Minerva are well represented at Corinium, as is the god of trade Mercury. The worship of local gods and goddesses such as the Sulivae (mother goddesses) and the Genii Cucullati (literally hooded spirits) continued to flourish. Carvings of the Genii Cucullati have been found at Cirencester, Lower Slaughter, Daglingworth, Wycomb and Whittington. Alongside the worship of classical and local gods the Empire brought with it exotic mystery religions such as Mithraisim.

The only religions frowned upon by Rome were those that apparently threatened the supremacy of the state such as Druidism and the emerging cult of Christianity. This accounted for the persecution of both sects.

By the end of the 3rd century, Christianity was attracting important converts culminating in the conversion of the Emperor Constantine the Great in 312 AD and it was his sons who made it the official religion of the empire. In the provinces, in particular in rural areas, the worship of the old gods continued and flourished.

A Romano-Celtic sculpture of the Sulivae from the Leauses, Cirencester (the area to the north-west of Lewis Lane). Judging from the number of surviving images the worship of the mother goddesses or Sulivae was one of the most popular religious cults in Corinium. The Sulivae were fertility goddesses and are often depicted in threes – a number sacred to the Celts. A number of the sculptures of mother goddesses and a dedication inscription were found together in the Ashcroft area of Cirencester in 1899, which suggests this was possibly the location of a temple dedicated to them.

Accession number B2047

```
R O T A S
O P E R A
T E N E T
A R E P O
S A T O R
```

The 'Acrostic' or word-square remains one of the Museum's most important and controversial objects. It is one of only eleven examples known from the Roman world. This famous graffito is scratched on to the surface of a piece of 2nd century wall plaster and is in the form of a palindrome. It was found during excavations of a Roman house in Victoria Road, Cirencester in 1868.

It is perhaps the single most important piece of evidence for the spread of Christianity in Roman Britain before the conversion of Constantine I.

There have been many attempts to explain the Acrostic. The most widely accepted view is that it is a secret Christian code, and dates to a period of persecution. The word 'Tenet' forms the sign of a cross and the letters form an anagram of 'Pater Noster' (our father), with an A and an O repeated twice. It therefore contains the first two words of the Lord's Prayer with the Alpha and Omega, referring to Christ as the 'Beginning and the End'.

Some scholars believe that it may be Judaic in origin and others that is was nothing more than a clever word-game.

Accession number B950

An artist's reconstruction of Corinium at its height in the mid 4th century AD based on the archaeological evidence.

Corinium Becomes a Provincial Capital: The End of Roman Britain

From 235 AD the Roman Empire was rocked by a half century of civil war, pandemics and barbarian invasion, with no fewer than 26 emperors ruling during that time. Britain was not immune from this civil strife and was twice part of a break away Empire, first as part of the so-called Gallic Empire (AD 260-74) and then under its own Emperor, Carausius (AD 286-293).

At the beginning of the 4th century, in an attempt to stabilize the Empire, the Emperor Diocletian divided it into 12 regions or Dioceses and these were subdivided into provinces. Britain was divided into four provinces; with capitals at Londinium (London), Lindum (Lincoln), Eburacum (York) and Corinium (Cirencester). Corinium was the capital of Britannia Prima which encompassed the whole of south-western Britain and Wales.

The 4th century was a period of great prosperity for Roman Britain with many fine villas and estates being rebuilt, but by the end of the century many of its towns were in decline. As a provincial capital Corinium was different; its occupation actually peaked about 350 AD. It is probable that a new palace for the Governor and a church for the Christian bishop of the province were built at this time. Certainly the Basilica Forum complex was extensively remodelled and a number of large town houses were built or refurbished, including the Beeches Road house.

Elsewhere, parts of the town were deliberately cleared of buildings; possibly for the stockpiling of taxes in kind (the *Annona*), such as cattle, grain and leather, and the town's defences were modified by adding external towers or bastions.

An extremely rare gold Aureus of the Emperor Carausius. The obverse bears a rather thug-like portrait of the Emperor, presumably how he wished to be seen. At a time when he was at war with the rest of the Empire this coin bears the somewhat ironic reverse inscription PAX AVG (peace of the emperor). This coin was struck in London but it is probable that Carausius had also set up a mint at Corinium.

Accession number 1979/40/8

The Romans • 18/19

A fine gold Solidus of the Emperor Honorius (383-423 AD) found at Cirencester. The solidus was struck at 1/72 of a Roman pound (about 4.5 grams). Archaeology shows us that coins were being used as widely and as frequently in Roman Cirencester in the 390's AD as they had been in the 330's, which is a remarkable testament to the town's economic resilience to the end of the Roman period. In 402 AD, Honorius retired to the inaccessible and heavily defended city of Ravenna. It was from there, in 410 AD, he wrote to the cities of Roman Britain telling them to look to their own defences.

Accession number 2002/10

The collapse of the Rhine frontier and the fall of Roman Gaul (France) to Germanic invaders in 407 AD effectively severed Britain from political and military contact with the rest of the Empire. Corinium, dependent on the political and economic structures of the Roman Empire, collapsed and its inhabitants apparently drifted away to the countryside.

An artist's reconstruction of the Beeches Road town house at the end of the 4th century AD. One of the two Beeches Road town houses had 21 rooms with five mosaic floors and two hypocausts, whereas the other had 16 rooms and no less than 12 mosaics and five hypocausts. The largest of its three barns had been partitioned off to provide low status accommodation, presumably for the farm labourers.

Septimius stone. This important inscription was found in Victoria Road Cirencester and records the restoration of a Jupiter column in the town by Lucius Septimius described as the Rector (governor) of the Province of Britannia Prima.

Accession number B952

The Anglo-Saxons

Invaders or Settlers

The collapse of Roman rule in Britain during the 5th century AD left a vacuum into which peoples from Northern Germany, Holland and Jutland migrated and settled here in increasing numbers. Although they were made up of a number of peoples including the Jutes, Frisians, Saxons and Angles, they are generally known today as the Anglo-Saxons. These people introduced a new way of life, culture and language which were to completely supplant those that had gone before.

The richest grave in the early cemetery was that of a young woman, aged 25-30 years old, who the archaeologists nicknamed *Mrs. Getty* because of the wealth and number of her grave goods. Her burial dates to the 6th century AD and is one of the richest Anglo-Saxon burials ever found in Britain. Her grave is unusual not only for its wealth but also in that she was buried in a wooden coffin, another indication of her importance.

Accession number 1997/25/18

The Anglo-Saxons · 20/21

Reconstruction of "Mrs. Getty" from grave 18 Butler's Field, Lechlade. This was the richest 6th century grave in the cemetery and contained a woman 24-30 years old who was buried in a stone lined grave and in a wooden coffin. Her importance to the community is further indicated by the fact her grave contained over 200 finds. Her skull and face has been forensically reconstructed so that you can literary gaze on the face of an Anglo-Saxon princess!

Saxons from North West Germany seem to have been the main settlers in the Thames valley and from there spread onto the Cotswold Hills. Archaeological evidence for their settlements is rare. The early Saxons were pagan and buried their dead with grave goods and most of our knowledge about them comes from excavations of their cemeteries. A number of important early Saxon examples are known from the western end of the Thames valley, in particular at Fairford, Cirencester and Kemble.

The largest and most important of these sites is the cemetery at Butler's Field, Lechlade. This burial ground was in continuous use from the late 5th to the early 8th centuries AD and contained the remains of 248 men, women and children. There were two main phases of burials, the first and "pagan" lasted from about AD 450 to AD 600 and has graves orientated north-south. The second dates to the 7th and early 8th centuries, a time when Christianity was becoming the dominant religion in England. Although the 57 graves from this phase are orientated east-west, as is usual for Christians, many still contained grave goods, which implies the locals were hedging their bets. Butler's Field remains the only Anglo-Saxon cemetery in the Thames Valley where 'pagan' and 'Christian' burials occupy the same site.

At first, the Saxons of Lechlade maintained links to their homelands. The huge quantity of Baltic amber beads from the 6th century graves shows a continuing trade between the Cotswolds and Scandinavia. Likewise finds of a number of metal bowls and cauldrons from the Rhineland hints at links with northern Germany.

The graves of only 50 men were found at Butler's Field, while those of women numbered 89. The richest and perhaps most important male grave was that of a 16-18 year old. He was buried sometime between AD 475 and AD 550 with a shield, two spears, a knife and a cauldron, and like *Mrs. Getty*, he was also buried in a wooden coffin.

Accession number 1997/25/92

These four rare and beautiful gold pendants were found in graves at the Butler's Field Anglo-Saxon cemetery and date to the 7th century AD. The Anglo-Saxons were famed for their metal-working skills and looking at these pendants it is easy to see why.

Two were found with women aged 35-40 and two with young children aged 2-4 years old. While they were highly prized objects they were not kept locked out of sight. The signs of wear show they were worn regularly if not everyday.

Accession numbers 1997/25/84/3; 1997/25/95/1/1; 1997/25/179/3; 1997/25/172/2/12

During the next century, the pattern of trade altered. The 7th century graves contain luxury goods such as cowrie shells and objects decorated with garnets and amethysts. These indicate trade with the Mediterranean which in turn gave access to goods from the Indian Ocean.

Early Saxon settlements are rare in Britain and little can be said with certainty even about Saxon Cirencester.

A gilt bronze keystone garnet disc brooch. Amongst the interlace are four circular and four triangular settings. The two remaining flat circular insets and the larger domed white central setting would appear to be shell. The triangular insets are garnets, laid on cross-hatched gold foil. Found with the body of a child aged 4 to 5 in grave 17 during excavations at an Anglo-Saxon cemetery at Butler's Field, Lechlade.

Accession number 1997/25/17

However in 1997 part of a large settlement, contemporary with the Butler's Field cemetery, was discovered in Lechlade. Excavations revealed six small buildings with sunken floors, either houses or workshops, which suggest a modest community surviving on its local resources in complete contrast to the exotic wealth of their burials.

During the 7th and 8th centuries, Cirencester and the Cotswolds remained a disputed border area between the contending kingdoms of Mercia and Wessex. Following the defeat of the Danes by Alfred the Great at the battle of Ethandune (Edington) in 878, Guthrum the Danish leader came to Cirencester where the Anglo-Saxon Chronicle records, "the Danes remained a whole year".

The Anglo-Saxons • 22/23

Among the grave goods from Butler's Field are several objects connected with the production of wool and woollen cloth, such as shears and combs, spindle whorls and weaving battens that may hold the key to the commodity that the people at Butler's Field were exchanging for their luxury items. Wool!

Accession number 1997/25/14; 1997/25/54; 1997/25/66; 1997/25/81; 1997/25/187

In the late Saxon period Cirencester became the centre of a Royal estate, where the King occasionally held his council. In 999 Ethelred the Unready issued a charter from Cirencester ordering the banishment of an important local earl, Aelfric for an unspecified crime, and at Easter in 1020, King Cnut held a Great Council in the town. However with the exception of the remains of an impressive stone parish church, with the longest Saxon nave in England, built sometime between the late 7th and mid 10th centuries, evidence for the late Saxon settlement is sparse.

The "Tunley Torc". This 9th or early 10th century plaited gold Anglo-Norse ring was found at Tunley, Gloucestershire in 1872. Sadly no other evidence was recovered with it. A reminder of this turbulent period, was it Saxon or Viking plunder or simply hidden by a wealthy local from both sides? We shall never know!

Accession number 1971/1

The Medieval Period

Abbots & Flocks

The Norman Conquest of England in 1066 had little immediate effect on the Cotswolds, other than a change in master. Cirencester itself remained a Royal estate and in the Domesday survey is listed as having only 56 adult inhabitants and 3 mills. A market was granted to the manor in 1086 to be held on a Sunday, but the terms of the charter of Richard I (1157-1199) granted markets on Mondays and Fridays instead. These markets are still held today!

Excavations carried out in the Abbey Grounds just behind the Parish Church in 1964 and 1965 revealed the plan of the abbey church and a wealth of broken sculpture from the chapter house including these 15th century Abbot's and Pope's heads. The quality of the workmanship hints at the lost glories of the Abbey and its buildings, sculpture and stained glass.

Abbot's head accession number 1980/79/31. Pope's head accession number 1980/79/30

A quarter rose gold noble of Edward III (1330-1377) found at Barton Farm, Cirencester, one of the farms of St. Mary's Abbey. During the 14th century a gold exchange was established in Cirencester market place next to the Boothall, on the site of the present Corn Hall.

Accession number A85

Over the next three hundred years Cirencester changed from a farming community to an increasingly important centre of trade. The Poll Tax return of 1381 lists 574 men and women, some are still agricultural labourers but the majority now have other occupations. These include merchants, tailors, goldsmiths, blacksmiths, braziers, brewers, innkeepers and cooks, servants, seamstresses, stallholders, a saddler, maltsters, masons and a mustard maker.

The most important industry in Cirencester was the manufacture of woollen cloth. By the middle of the 13th century, the dyeing of cloth was such an important occupation that *Cheaping* (market) Street was renamed Dyer Street. In the 12th and 13th centuries the English wool trade flourished and Cotswold wool was much sought after. Fine churches and cathedrals were built with money earned from this trade and many abbeys, including St. Mary's Cirencester, had their own flocks. By the 14th and 15th centuries the trade, in Cotswold wool was on an international scale. Francesco Datini, an important Italian merchant from Prato, stated that *"the best wool in Europe came from the Cotswolds and the best wool in the Cotswolds came from Cirencester"*.

The goods offered for sale in the market itself became more exotic. The tolls for 1321 list silk and cloth of gold amongst 80 other items: Amongst the luxury items bought there, may have been this elephant ivory knife handle in the form of a Lady with a hawk. It was probably carved in Paris in the early 14th century and was found in the Old Ship Inn, Dyer Street, Cirencester in 1900.

Accession number G55

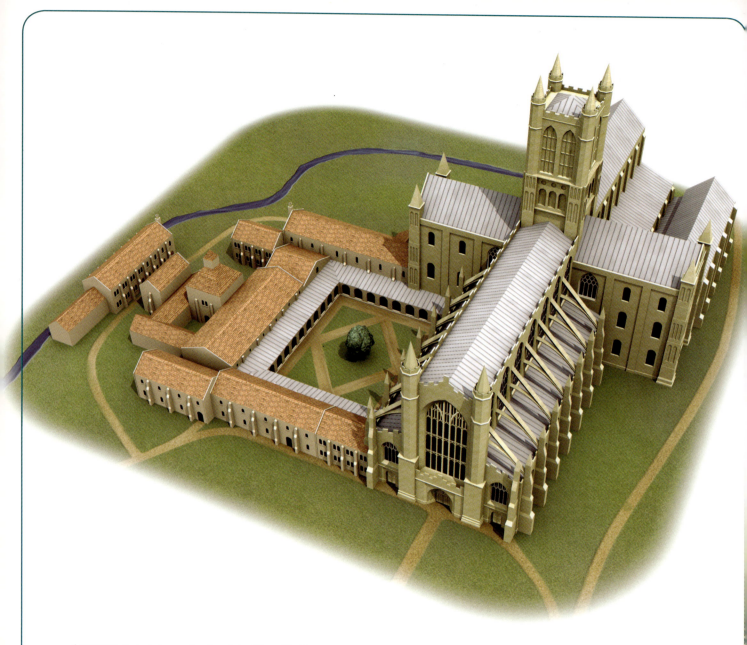

A computer generated reconstruction of the Abbey of St. Mary based upon the excavated evidence, contemporary descriptions and surviving Augustinian churches. The Abbey Church was about one and a half times the length of the Parish Church and the precincts, which housed only 40 canons, contained the religious buildings, two farms, dovecotes, orchards, mills and gardens. The conventual (religious) buildings consisted of the Abbey Church itself, a chapter house and cloisters, a library, and a muniment room for the storing of robes. There was also a refectory (dining hall) for the monks with kitchens and latrines, an infirmary, and an inn for poor travellers and pilgrims. All that now remains is the Spital Gate.

The Medieval Period · 26/27

Late Medieval interest in the instruments of Christ's passion was fostered by the belief that large indulgences could be gained by devotions performed in their presence. The emblems or selections of them were conveniently available as hat badges. The cross, crown of thorns, three nails, spear, reed sceptre, the cock that crowed, dice, the pillar and scourges appear in a neatly symmetrical arrangement on this stamped brass disc. Circa 1500, excavated at Cirencester Abbey in 1965.

Accession number 1980/79/14

Perhaps the most significant event effecting the development of the medieval and later town was the founding of the great Augustinian Abbey of St. Mary. It dominated the lives of the people of Cirencester for over 400 years. Building work began in 1117 and continued unabated until the 16th century, as successive Abbots extended and beautified the Abbey.

As lords of the manor, the Abbots controlled all aspects of life in the town. They owned and developed properties throughout Cirencester, particularly in Abbot's (now Coxwell) Street and around the Market Place. When St. Mary's Abbey was dissolved in 1539 it owned 152 houses in Cirencester, its annual income was over £1,050 (£326,013 at current rates) and its other lands were valued at £132,607 (over £40,784,609 in today's money).

Medieval lead Ampulla. Ampullae or miniature phials were an important pilgrim souvenir. They were designed to contain holy water and were provided with a pair of handles so that they could be hung around the wearer's neck. This Ampulla probably dates to the period 1350-1530 and is from an unidentified shrine. Metal-detecting find from Lower End, Eastington.

Accession number 2007/20

The Tudors
New times, New men

The accession of the Tudor monarchy once again heralded changes in Cirencester's fortunes. In the 1530's, Henry VIII's marriage difficulties led to a break with the Pope and the Roman Catholic Church and the suppression of the monasteries and confiscation of their property.

Portrait of John Coxwell (1516-1614) a Cirencester wool merchant.

The Tudors • 28/29

A silver hammered groat (two-pence) of Henry VIII (1509-47). This coin struck between 1526 and 1532 in London bears a young but already heavy jowled portrait. On the obverse he styles himself King of England and France presaging his military adventures in that country. It was combination of Henry's break with Rome and his need for money to fund his military spending that led to the dissolution of the monasteries including Cirencester Abbey.

← *Portrait of John Coxwell (1516-1614) a Cirencester wool merchant. John Coxwell, a self made local man who made his money from the wool trade, typifies this process. He rose from the ranks of the lower middle classes to that of the gentry. John was in his early twenties when Cirencester Abbey was dissolved but twenty years later, when Elizabeth I sold off the Abbey lands he was able to purchase a significant part. Eventually he owned over 40 properties in Cirencester. In 1563 he purchased part of the manor of Siddington, ten years later he bought the manor of Ablington. His new manor house there was complete by 1590 and the following year he acquired the manor of West Chelworth from the Duttons of Sherbourne. At his death in 1614 he held lands in Cirencester, Frampton, Bisley, Abness, Minchinhampton, Stroud, Baunton, Stratton, and Preston.*

Accession number 2002/41

Abbott John Blake surrendered Cirencester Abbey in December 1539. The King ordered the Abbey to be destroyed. Lead was stripped from the buildings and the Abbey's treasures sold. The dissolution of the monasteries had far reaching social effects. The sale of their estates allowed the gentry to extend their land holdings, and the middle classes to join the ranks of the gentry. Early in her reign, Elizabeth I conferred Oakley Manor, now Cirencester Park, on her treasurer Sir Thomas Parry and sold the Abbey estate to Richard Master, her physician. Like the Abbey before them these two estates dominated the lives of the people of the town. The political stability of Elizabeth I's reign boosted trade. This brought prosperity to the merchant classes, many of whom built new "manor" houses throughout the Cotswolds.

Silver gilt dress hook from Northleach. As the rising Cotswold middle classes established themselves socially and financially they started to imitate the court styles of dress and jewellery, although in a deliberately less ostentatious manner. This object is typical of the period and of the desire for conspicuous consumption whilst not falling foul of the Elizabethan 'sumptuary laws' (dress codes!).

Accession number 2006/43

The Civil War

For King or Parliament

At the beginning of the 17th century the Cotswolds witnessed both economic decline and the stirrings of social unrest. A dramatic collapse in the wool trade, occasioned by a combination of war raging on the continent, and irresponsible Royal fiscal policies, had a disastrous and long-lasting impact on Cirencester, where at least 18% of the population was still dependent upon this trade for their livelihood. These effects were also felt widely in the other wool towns of the county where not only the poor, but also the merchant classes suffered.

A Civil War pamphlet. This is a contemporary copy of the petition for clemency presented to the King on behalf of the people of Cirencester. It contains the names of many prominent townsfolk and was printed at the express order of the King in 1643. The English Civil War was amongst the first conflicts in Europe where the printing press was used extensively to win the propaganda war.

Accession number 2002/40

The Civil War

A carved shale silhouette of Endymion Porter (1587-1649). Porter was an important Royalist. A courtier and friend of Charles I. He was born in Mickleton and lived at Aston-sub-Edge near Chipping Campden. Porter was a patron of the Arts and helped found the Royal art collection.

Accession number 1999/36

By the 1630's political and religious opinion in Gloucestershire was increasingly polarized and there was open opposition to the personal rule of Charles I.

When war finally broke out between the King and Parliament in 1642, the kingdom was plunged into turmoil. The people of Cirencester, led by a number of prominent citizens, declared for Parliament and established a formidable garrison. Due to their strategic central position, the Cotswolds were fought over throughout the Civil Wars and Cirencester, at the junction of three major roads, was the key to its control. On the 2nd of February 1643 Prince Rupert launched a successful attack on the town. Over 300 defenders were killed and 1,200 prisoners were taken and marched to prison in Oxford. The town was ransacked and wool, cattle, sheep and horses were seized.

The Museum holds two important civil war coin hoards one from Ashbrook (Ampney St. Mary) and the most recent from Weston-sub-Edge, both are eloquent testimony to the disastrous economic and social effects of the war. The war brought financial ruin to many in Gloucestershire and near famine conditions to parts of the County. Throughout the war, the Cotswolds suffered from the repeated passage of armies, enforced billeting and seizure of property and possessions.

The Weston-sub-Edge Hoard.
This large and important Civil War hoard consists of 307 silver and 2 gold coins. It was found under the floor of a former barn in Weston-sub-Edge in 1981. The coins were contained in a specially made lead pipe and were accompanied by a scrap of paper which declared "Ye Hoard is £18". Who buried this money we shall never know but what is certain is that they were never able to recover it!

Accession number 1984/7/3-311

18/19th Centuries

Eighteenth and Nineteenth Century Cirencester

Cirencester had recovered from the effects of the Civil War by the early 18th century, as had its major industry, the wool trade. Daniel Defoe, who visited Cirencester in 1724, comments; *"Cirencester is still a very good town, populous and rich, full of clothiers, and driving a great trade in wool"*. However, by the late 18th century, cloth manufacture was concentrated in the Stroud valleys, on sites with easy access to water to power the mills.

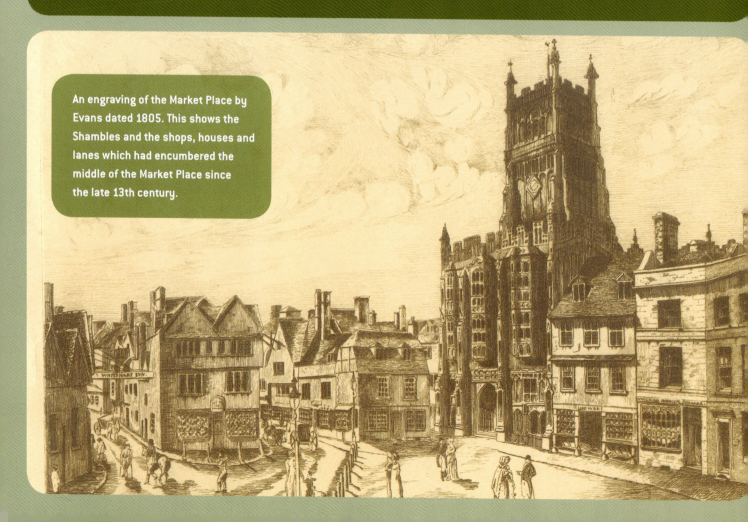

An engraving of the Market Place by Evans dated 1805. This shows the Shambles and the shops, houses and lanes which had encumbered the middle of the Market Place since the late 13th century.

18/19th Centuries • 32/33

A cased silver pocket watch. This watch was made by Coates of Cirencester, a maker noted for the high quality of his workmanship. Coates appears to have had premises in Dyer Street, Cirencester. The case is inscribed with the owner's name Francis Gibbs and the date 1771.

Accession number 2004/33

Inevitably trade in Cirencester declined, with only one mill, New Mills, continuing to operate until the early 19th century. The dwindling cloth trade was replaced with the manufacture of tools for agricultural implements and machinery, and a mixed farming economy.

The Industrial Revolution arrived in Cirencester by canal. The Cirencester arm of the Thames and Severn Canal opened in 1789. The 18th century also brought an expansion of social life. The Cirencester Flying Post newspaper started, the playing of cricket began, and a theatre opened in Gloucester Street.

In the 19th century parts of the private estates, which had hemmed the town into its historic medieval core, were sold off and developed, and the town doubled its size and population.

With development on the margins, the centre of the town could be relieved of pressure. Expansion of residential housing began after 1826 with the sale of Watermoor Common and housing construction along Watermoor Road and Stepstairs Lane. This meant that by 1830 the Market Place could be cleared of its cluster of buildings leaving the view almost as you see it today.

As the town developed, the processing of locally produced goods came to be an important factor. The Corn Hall opened in 1862 enabling the corn dealers to transact their business under cover for the first time. As commerce expanded so did the accompanying infrastructure with a number of private and commercial banks being founded at the end of the century.

Today Cirencester remains a vibrant market town with a strong sense of its own identity and with a wealth of historic buildings built in the mellow local limestone for you to enjoy. Please stay a while and explore its many treasures!

Mourning ring. An exquisite gold and enamel mourning ring inscribed Elizabeth Lodge and dated January 1776.

Accession number G266

The Corinium Museum

A brief history

The Corinium Museum owes its origins to two private family collections: those of the Bathursts and the Cripps. The first Corinium Museum founded by the 4th Earl Bathurst opened in 1856 to house recent discoveries and the building still stands in Tetbury Road, although no longer a museum.

A bronze seal cube from the Roman small town at Kingscote near Tetbury. Five of its six faces are engraved with symbols associated with the imperial court, and are personifications of Rome, the unconquered sun (Sol Invictus), Mars, Concord, sol in a quadriga (four horsed chariot). The final face is engraved with a scene of hunting. Late 3rd century AD.

Accession number 1998/96/7/1

The Corinium Museum • 34/35

An engraving of the first Corinium Museum. In 1856 the 4th Earl Bathurst had a museum built into the wall of Cirencester Park to house his collections of antiquities. This was open daily to the public.

This private collection together with the Cripps Collection were given to the town in 1936 to form the second Corinium Museum and the first one to be established on the present site in Park Street. The new purpose-built museum was erected in the grounds of Abberley House, a grade 2 listed building, and was opened in 1938.

Between 1972 and 1974 the Cirencester Urban District Council redeveloped the Museum, but as part of local government reorganisation in Gloucestershire in 1974, the Museum was transferred to the ownership of Cotswold District Council. Since then the Museum has functioned as a section of that authority. Cotswold District Council has maintained and expanded the collections acquiring important archaeological material from all over the District, including the Cirencester Excavation Committee's Roman and Medieval archive from the excavations in the town between 1959 and 1974 and the nationally important Saxon cemetery from Butler's Field, Lechlade.

Between 2002 and 2004, with the support of the Heritage Lottery Fund, Cotswold District Council undertook an ambitious redevelopment project of the entire Museum, to take it into the 21st century.

A contemporary engraving showing the lifting of the Hunting Dogs Mosaic in 1849. It was the discovery of this mosaic and the Seasons Mosaic, during sewage works in Dyer Street, which gave rise to the establishment of the first Corinium Museum.

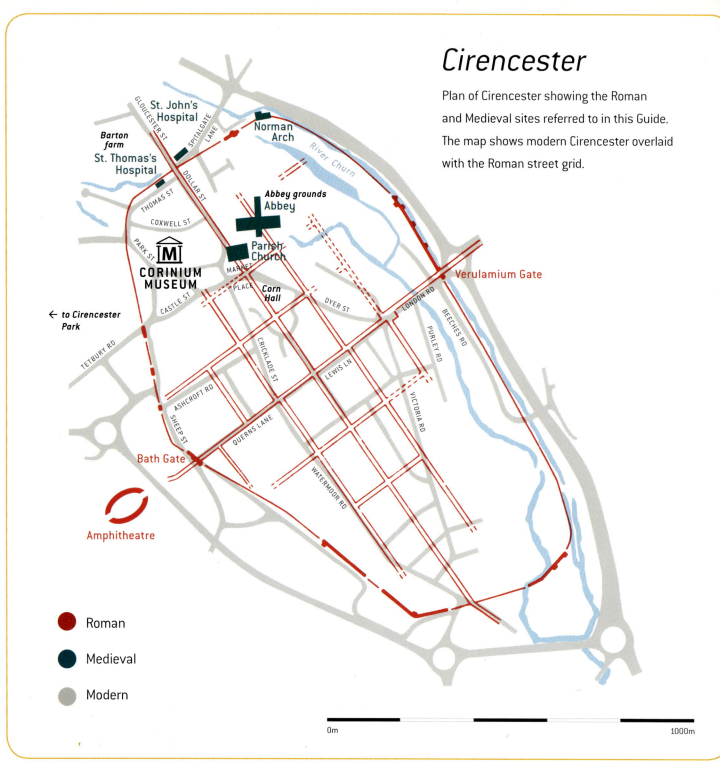